I0879474

The Go[illegible]

Akron Series in Poetry

Winner of the 2001 Akron Poetry Prize

ALSO BY GEORGE BILGERE

Big Bang

The Going

AKRON SERIES IN POETRY

Elton Glaser, Editor

Barry Seiler, *The Waters of Forgetting*
Raeburn Miller, *The Comma After Love: Selected Poems of Raeburn Miller*
William Greenway, *How the Dead Bury the Dead*
Jon Davis, *Scrimmage of Appetite*
Anita Feng, *Internal Strategies*
Susan Yuzna, *Her Slender Dress*
Raeburn Miller, *The Collected Poems of Raeburn Miller*
Clare Rossini, *Winter Morning with Crow*
Barry Seiler, *Black Leaf*
William Greenway, *Simmer Dim*
Jeanne E. Clark, *Ohio Blue Tips*
Beckian Fritz Goldberg, *Never Be the Horse*
Marlys West, *Notes for a Late-Blooming Martyr*
Dennis Hinrichsen, *Detail from* The Garden of Earthly Delights
Susan Yuzna, *Pale Bird, Spouting Fire*
John Minczeski, *Circle Routes*
Barry Seiler, *Frozen Falls*
Melody Lacina, *Private Hunger*
George Bilgere, *The Good Kiss*
William Greenway, *Ascending Order*

The Good Kiss

Poems by

George Bilgere

The University of Akron Press
Akron, Ohio

Copyright © 2002 by George Bilgere

Some of the poems in this volume have appeared in or are forthcoming in the following journals: *Atlanta Review:* "Annulment" (published as "Anniversary"); *Denver Quarterly:* "Ike"; *Field:* "Stupid," "Jennifer," "Cordell"; *The Journal:* "Old Man River"; *Missouri Review:* "Pain," "Eden," "Nectarines," "Anywhere"; *Ploughshares*: "The Good Kiss" (published as "Almost the Same"); *Sewanee Review:* "Like Riding a Bicycle," "Laundry," "Let Down"; *Southern Review:* "Crusoe," "Threepenny Opera"; *Tar River Poetry:* "Corned Beef and Cabbage," "The Garage," "Satisfied."

All rights reserved. First Edition 2002.
11 10 09 5 4

All inquiries and permissions requests should be addressed to the publisher,
The University of Akron Press, Akron, OH 44325–1703

Library of Congress Cataloging-in-Publication Data

Bilgere, George, 1951—
The good kiss : poems / by George Bilgere.— 1st ed.
p. cm. — (Akron series in poetry)
ISBN 1-884836-92-5 (alk. paper) — ISBN 1-884836-93-3 (pbk. : alk. paper)
I. Title. II. Series.
PS3552.I425 G66 2002
811'.54—DC21
2002014834

Manufactured in the United States of America.
The paper used in this publication meets the minimum requirements of American National Standard for Information Sciences—Permanence of Paper for Printed Library Materials, ANSI Z39.48–1984. ∞

Cover painting: Edvard Munch: *The Kiss* 1892, Oil on canvas 73 x 92 cm, National Gallery, Oslo. Artwork © Munch Museum/Munch-Ellingsen Group/ARS 2007. Photo © Munch Museum (Andersen/de Jong).

Contents

For Cec

Like Riding a Bicycle

I would like to write a poem
About how my father taught me
To ride a bicycle one soft twilight,
A poem in which he was tired
And I was scared, unable to disbelieve
In gravity and believe in him,
As the fireflies were coming out
And only enough light remained
For one more run, his big hand at the small
Of my back, pulling away like the gantry
At a missile launch, and this time, this time
I wobbled into flight, caught a balance
I would never lose, and pulled away
From him as he eased, laughing, to a stop,
A poem in which I said that even today
As I make some perilous adult launch,
Like pulling away from my wife
Into the fragile new balance of our life
Apart, I can still feel that steadying hand,
Still hear that strong voice telling me
To embrace the sweet fall forward
Into the future's blue
Equilibrium. But,

Of course, he was drunk that night,
Still wearing his white shirt
And tie from the office, the air around us
Sick with scotch, and the challenge
Was keeping his own balance
As he coaxed his bulk into a trot

Beside me in the hot night, sweat
Soaking his armpits, the eternal flame
Of his cigarette flaring as he gasped
And I fell, again and again, entangled
In my gleaming Schwinn, until
He swore and stomped off
Into the house to continue
Working with my mother
On their own divorce, their balance
Long gone and the hard ground already
Rising up to smite them
While I stayed outside in the dark,
Still falling, until at last I wobbled
Into the frail, upright delight
Of feeling sorry for myself, riding
Alone down the neighborhood's
Black street like the lonely western hero
I still catch myself in the act
Of performing.

And yet, having said all this,
I must also say that this summer evening
Is very beautiful, and I am older
Than my father ever was
As I coast the Pacific shoreline
On my old bike, the gears clicking
Like years, the wind
Touching me for the first time, it seems,
In a very long time,
With soft urgency all over.

Corned Beef and Cabbage

I can see her in the kitchen,
Cooking up, for the hundredth time,
A little something from her
Limited Midwestern repertoire.
Cigarette going in the ashtray,
The red wine pulsing in its glass,
A warning light meaning
Everything was simmering
Just below the steel lid
Of her smile, as she boiled
The beef into submission,
Chopped her way
Through the vegetable kingdom
With the broken-handled knife
I use tonight, feeling her
Anger rising from the dark
Chambers of the head
Of cabbage I slice through,
Missing her, wanting
To chew things over
With my mother again.

Crusoe

When you've been away from it long enough,
You begin to forget the country
Of couples, with all its strange customs
And mysterious ways. Those two
Over there, for instance: late thirties,
Attractive and well-dressed, reading
At the table, drinking some complicated
Coffee drink. They haven't spoken
Or even looked at each other in thirty minutes,

But the big toe of her right foot, naked
In its sandal, sometimes grazes
The naked ankle bone of his left foot,

The faintest signal, a line thrown

Between two vessels as they cruise
Through this hour, this vacation, this life,
Through the thick novels they're reading,
Her toe saying to his ankle,

Here's to the whole improbable story
Of our meeting, of our life together
And the oceanic richness
Of our mingled narrative
With its complex past, with its hurts
And secret jokes, its dark closets
And delightful sexual quirks,
Its occasional doldrums, its vast

Future we have already peopled
With children. How safe we are

Compared to that man sitting across the room,
Marooned with his drink
And yellow notebook, trying to write
A way off his little island.

Jennifer

I step naked into the backyard
Under a full moon
And piss on the rich soil
At the edge of the flower bed,

Feeling both Whitmanesque and doglike,
Mystical and silly.

When I was a kid, my friends and I
Would pee together, crossing
Yellow swords,
Seeing who could go longest and farthest.

And over the years,
Three or four women have asked shyly
If they could watch
What might have seemed to them
The essential male act: brutish
And comic, complexly hydraulic,
Full of archaic territoriality—

The one act of the penis
Over which we have more control
Than they do.

Maybe that's why,
When I walked home a little buzzed
From a Denver bar one winter night

With a girl I hardly knew
And desperately needing a convenient tree,

She took me in her cold hand
And wrote her own name in the snow.

Great Cathedrals

Before a date, my college roommate
Used to drive his candy-apple red Camaro
Down to the car wash and spend the afternoon
Washing, waxing, vacuuming it,
Detailing the chrome strips, buffing the fenders,
Spraying the big expensive tires
With their raised white lettering

That said something like *Intruder*
Or *Marauder*, with a silicone spray
Until they were slick and dark as sex.
He polished that car as if each caress,
Each pass of the chamois, each loving
Stroke of the terry cloth would increase,

By measurable degrees,
The likelihood that in the immaculate
Front seat, with its film of freshly applied
Vinyl cleaner, at the end of a cul-de-sac
Somewhere above the campus,
She would consent to be rubbed
And buffed just as lovingly.

We do what we can,
And if God is no more impressed
By the cathedral at Chartres
Than by a righteously clean and cherry
Camaro, at least He can't say
We haven't tried

With all our might to conceal our fear
That we have little else to offer
Than stained glass or polished chrome,
The elbow grease of our good intentions.

So I'm happy to see
That in the Christmas card photo he sent
Mark stands, balding now,
With a dignified gut, a pretty wife,
And a couple of nice-looking kids, in front
Of the great cathedral
Like the sweet vision of a future
He'd been vouchsafed one day
Long ago, through Turtle Wax
On a gleaming hubcap.

What I Want

for my marriage, 1996–2000

I want a good night's sleep.
I want to get up without feeling
That to waken is to plunge through a trap door.

I want to ride my motorcycle
In late spring through the Elysian Fields
Of the Rocky Mountains

And lie once more with Cecelia
In the summer of 1985
On a blanket in the backyard of our house

In Denver and watch the clouds expand.
And it would be great to see my mother
Alive again, at the stove, frying a pan of noodles

Into that peculiar carbonized disk that has never been replicated.
I would like for my ex-wife to get leprosy,
Her beauty falling away in little chunks

To the disgust of everyone in the chic café
Where she exercises her gift
For doing absolutely nothing.

I want world peace.
I want to come home one evening
And find that Julia, the new assistant professor

In the history department,
Has let herself into my apartment
For the express purpose of lecturing me

On the history of lingerie.
I don't ask for much: a good merlot.
An afternoon thunderstorm cooling off

The city as I sit listening to Ella
Sing "Spring is Here," so the air goes lyrical
And perhaps a stray bolt of lightning

Strikes my ex-wife as she steps from her car,
Setting her on fire, to the unqualified delight
Of the friends she has come to visit,

Who are thoroughly sick of her self-aggrandizing stories.
I want to spark a bowl of Maui Wowie
And spend the entire afternoon in my dorm room

With Corrine Spellman, trying to remember
What we were talking about, wondering
Whether, in fact, we had had sex yet.

I'd like to sit at the little outdoor restaurant
By the lake in Forest Park, talking with my aunt
In the humid summer twilight, as the hot

St. Louis day expires upon the water
And the moth-eaten Chinese lanterns
Glow like faded Kodachrome.

We would argue about the great tenor voices
Of the century, or causes for the dearth
Of poetry about the Gulf War,

Or why my father drank himself into an elegy
We never stop revising,
While couples on their paddleboats come in

From the darkening lake, as they've done
Since the beginning of time, and children
Call each other across the shadowy fields.

Yes, that would be nice.
I want a good woman
With a sweet bosom

And a wicked sense of humor.
I want to wake up in London on a spring morning
And read in the paper that my ex-wife

Has received a lethal injection, courtesy of the state
Of Ohio, as part of a citywide program aimed
At improving the civic pride of Cleveland,

But something went terribly wrong
And she's been left in a persistent
Vegetative state

Which everyone agrees
Is nonetheless an improvement.
And it would be wonderful

To sit down with Maria
At our favorite restaurant in Madrid
With some good red wine

And listen to her Spanish
Caress the evening.
I want to read that a new manuscript

Of poetry by James Wright
Has been discovered in someone's attic,
And someone I haven't yet met,

In some future I have yet to despoil,
Has bought it for my birthday,
And after the kids are asleep

We sit out in the backyard,
A little drunk, and read it
Aloud to each other,

Something we often do
In summer, before climbing upstairs to the bedroom
In the big old house we love so much.

Anywhere

The boy's been on the computer all morning
Playing virtual baseball, July
Sliding by in a huge yellow silence
Beyond the window as he clicks the keyboard

To send the phantom players running
The base paths under a virtual sky
In a nameless city's digital summer.

Naturally, I brood about this as I work
In the garage at fixing his bike's
Out-of-whack derailleur. *In my day,*
I find myself starting to say, before
My father's fossil phrase
Catches in my craw—

Better to speak with this tool in my hand,
This old-fashioned screwdriver,
Its Phillips head buried in the steel
Crux of the material world, the torque
Flowing from my old-fashioned wrist

So chain will rise from sprocket, and power
From a boy's legs will carry him from home
And down the afternoon street to nowhere
In particular, or anywhere: places
I used to head for on a summer day.

Magellan

When a beautiful woman lies down
On her brown belly, on her pink beach towel,
And reaches back and behind to perform
That curious legerdemain whereby
Her dazzling white
Bikini top is undone
And she stretches out under the sun,

I continue watching the breakers
Stagger to their knees, and listen
To the gulls work through
Their chronic desolation,
Thinking, for some reason,
Of my mother, struggling
Into the cross-stitched straitjacket
Of her girdle
Before a night out with my father,

And I think of the boundless
Surge and heave of the oceans,
Swollen and unfettered
Before any man, crazed
By indifferent beauty, raised
White sails to cup
The wind's breasts
And girdle the globe.

Tamed

This summer my nephew
Is old enough for his first job:
Mowing the lawn.

I watch him lean his skinny chest
To the bar of the pushmower,
Put his weight into it, and become,

For the first time, a beast in harness,
A laborer on the face of the earth,
Somehow withering and expanding at the same time

Into something worn and ancient, but still
A kid withal, and I remember
How bitterly I went into the traces,

Hating that Saturday ritual,
For a while, then growing inexplicably
Into it, gradually mastering

The topography of the yard,
Sometimes using the back and forth technique,
Sometimes going for the checkerboard effect,

Or my favorite, the ever-diminishing square
That left, at the lawn's center, one
Last uncut stand of grass, a wild fortress

I annihilated with a strange thrill,
Then stood back to take a look—
To survey the field. To cast

A critical eye on my work.
Just as this kid is doing, standing
At the edge of the mowed clearance.

Taking his own measure. And liking it.

Eden

When Sarah and Jill, after a few years
Together, decided Sarah should become a man,
They thought about it for a long time,

Staring at Sarah's breasts in the candlelight
As they hung dejectedly
Like a pair of old dogs
Someone decided to put to sleep.

And they looked between her legs
At that wild gate that was like the first sentence
Of a story they had grown tired of telling.

They seemed to hear a kind of music
Under the surface of her skin, a far-off joy—
And years later, after the hormones and the stitches,
The lopping and relocating,

I met a slim, serious young guy
Who had been Sarah
At a cocktail party in Monterey,
And we shook hands and had a couple of beers

While I smiled and tried very hard not to feel
As if a woman had slit open the sack
Of my scrotum and crawled inside,
Confidently palming my testicles in her strong hands,
Saying, *There will be no more*
Secrets around here.

Westward Ho

I drive up and down the same five- or six-mile stretch
Of coastline north of Santa Cruz, the sun
Just about to touch down
On the heads of surfers waiting for a last good ride.

Johnny Cash is on the tape deck
For no particular reason, but the songs seem
To bend and straighten with the road,
Their rhythm following the coast's.

I love this, the way the car and the music
Go together with the way the road
And the ocean go together, joining
In this strange pleasure, this thing called
Cruising, this lovely way of wasting time

That only humans of the twentieth century
Could know, and I think of the wagonmasters
Leading their convoys of Conestogas
Over Kansas and Wyoming and Nevada,
Feeling the thrill and the dread
Of the oceanic emptiness full of savages,
The ice-locked mountain ranges
Where some of them would famously
Eat each other, and beyond it all

The green promise of the Pacific,
A glitter in the mind that kept them moving
Across that vastness into John Ford westerns

Unreeling through the insomniac hours.
They couldn't have imagined

This drive up and down the coast, their long
Westward haul detoured, stymied, turned inward
Into a daydream, a sad love song, rising
Like an elegy for all ended journeys
Above the postcard bay and beyond
The windshield, the ocean flashing on my left
While in the houses on my right
The TVs are flickering into prime time,
And married couples, becalmed at the end

Of the day, of the wild journey
That got them here, sit down
In front of their screens.

St. Paul's

Dwells with me still mine irksome memory
Which, both to keepe, and lose, grieves equally.
—John Donne

Sitting at St. Paul's,
Listening to the word of God,
I try to imagine what it would be like
To hear John Donne up there,
Cleaning up his act to a packed house,
Listing the pros and cons of this world,
Weighing the odds against entering the next—

And my mind drifts back to a summer evening
At Fairmont Lake, parked by the shore with someone
Named Barbara, watching the lights
Of the little electric boats, red and green,
My arm around her shoulders
As couples navigated the dark waters.

Sitting on my stone-cold pew
Like an errant thought
In the mind of Christopher Wren, I realize
That I would rather be back there
In the front seat of my mother's bargelike Bonneville
With Barbara, weighing the odds against
Unbuttoning her blouse—

And knowing what I know
Of John Donne, I'm guessing
He'd rather be there, too, mystified
By the green-eyed radio and Sam Cooke

Doing "Saturday Night," but entranced
By Barbara and the plush velour bench seat,
The glassed-in room, cozy as a sonnet
He'd write about our failure to be serious
At growing old; time, he would argue,

Will drag us presently from the warm car
And Barbara and the boat-lit summer
And into the cold cathedral,
So for God's sake hold your tongue
And let me love.

Elegy for the LP

There, in the twilight,
A long-necked bird
Lowers its head
And dark beak
To drink
So deeply
From the flowing river.

When at last it looks up
To see me watching,
Saddened and amazed,
The woods grow silent again.
For a long time,
We both sit very still.

Let Down

We're sitting on the deck at the day's end,
Drinks melting into the redwood table,
The fresh green lawn lapping at our feet.

This early dusk has all the ease
Of a tense muscle letting go, of the unexpected,
Delicious release I sometimes feel, deep down,
When I pass a beautiful woman.

The day is letting its pent-up kindness
Descend upon me, upon my sister and her husband
Whose marriage sails on imperturbably
Through the mild squall they're having

Just now over the small and beautiful
Problem of when to sell the stock options.
My own marriage has foundered, gone down
Somewhere beyond the green gulf of lawn. Her chair

From past summers when we sat here
Sits alone, in dry dock, over by the fence,
Disgraced somehow, as if it had let us down,
As if it had failed to deliver her,

With her unexpected laughter
And torrent of black hair
She used to let down on me
With a smile, when the day had let down

Its darkness, and I think of how
A nursing woman lets down her milk,
Something a man cannot imagine
But tries to imagine, and how

I let her down gently, but so often
That finally she let me down hard,
Leaving only three chairs drawn together
Against the night. And now Niel goes in

To file a late report, and Merry
Goes in to read aloud to her boys.
I sit out for another hour
In her chair.

Night Flight

I am doing laps at night, alone
In the indoor pool. Outside
It is snowing, but I am warm
And weightless, suspended and out
Of time like a fly in amber.

She is thousands of miles
From here, and miles above me,
Ghosting the stratosphere,
Heading from New York to London.
Though it is late, even
At that height, I know her light
Is on, her window a square
Of gold as she reads mysteries
Above the Atlantic. I watch

The line of black tile on the pool's
Floor, leading me down the lane.
If she looks down by moonlight,
Under a clear sky, she will see
Black water. She will see me
Swimming distantly, moving far
From shore, suspended with her
In flight through the wide gulf
As we swim toward land together.

Stupid

We were so fucked up,
She says to her friend, laughing.
We were so fucked up, it was. . . .
It was like. . . .
And her friend says, *Yeah,*
We totally were,

And I wonder
What it would be like
To be permanently stupid,
To go through life
At that altitude, just clearing
The lowest rooftops and TV aerials,
Heading for the mountains. . . .

My friends and I used to try it,
Sitting around a Day-Glo bong, brains
Turned to low, then lower,
So unmoored and adrift,
So hopelessly out of range
Of our calls to the lost
Vessels of each other,

We could only giggle, wondering,
Even as we did so,
Why.

Now and then,

The crippled sub of an idea
Would try to surface out there
On the stoned moment's
Glassy horizon

Where the strawberry-scented candle
Burned like. . . .

Like. . . .

The Garage

On these summer nights, I play
Ping-Pong with my brother-in-law,
A couple of beers sweating
On the tool shelf, the Giants game
Coming in loud and clear
On the paint-spattered shop radio,
And tonight I'm working very seriously
On my troublesome forehand,
Giving more concentration than usual
To the problem of topspin.

Today a woman on our street,
Running late for work, backed up
Her SUV and rolled over
Her three-year-old son. All day,
I've thought of her as she goes
Through the hours, living in that remote,
Astonishing place she has discovered,
Someplace wholly new
Where few of us have ever ventured,
And as I trot down the driveway
To retrieve an errant smash,
I realize that the sheer speed and pressure
Of her passage out of the world
I'm living in tonight, and into the blazing
Spaces where she is traveling
Far beyond me, like the blue fleck

Of a satellite, utterly alone,
Is what makes the lighted mouth
Of the garage, with its beer and ball game,
Its smell of oil and gas, its cardboard boxes
Of family history, seem like a sweet
Refuge, a cave I return to gratefully,

Holding the white moon of the ball—
A fragile, weightless thing.

Nectarines

The gay man standing next to me
At the organic food store
Is squeezing the nectarines
With the same concentration
I would give a woman's breasts,
Or he would give,
Or might give—I don't really know—
The weight between his lover's legs.

He is trim, fortyish, wearing a pair
Of vaguely European loafers
And the kind of perfect haircut
No stylist has ever felt I deserved.
His slacks and T-shirt exist at a point
On the spectrum of casual elegance
Just beyond my ability to actually detect it
But which nonetheless makes me feel,
In my jeans and JC Penney's sports shirt,
Like a shambling, half-trained circus bear.

When standing next to a woman
In a supermarket, I sometimes feel
As if we were back in the Garden,
A realm of fertile ferment
Where we walk in a kind of heady sexual buzz
Among the ripe fruits and frozen dinners of the world,
Temptation everywhere
As we scan the zebra codes
Of our deliciously
Unfamiliar flesh.

And when I pass a straight guy
In the aisles, we nod, or raise an eyebrow
To acknowledge our place
In the hairy fellowship of predators.

But when this man and I
Look briefly into the Sanskrit, the blank
Scrabble tiles of each other's eyes,
We smile briefly and go back
To thinking, quite seriously,
Of nectarines.

Threepenny Opera

The elderly modern dance instructor
And his elderly wife are dancing
In top hats and tails, doing a Kurt Weill
Number as old as their marriage.

They've reached that age when the body
Is starting to wonder how it got here,
When it has become strange, even to itself,
And moves around uncertainly
As if looking for a lost pair of glasses.

They do not mean for what they're doing
To be a parody, but, of course, it is;
The word means something like
"To sing alongside," and it's just
Possible to see the lithe dark lovers
They used to be, singing just beyond
The penumbra of the spotlight.
When they tap dance and set
Their old skeletons clattering

Across the stage, the teenage boy
In front of me smiles and nudges his girlfriend
Who has reached the moment
Of her beauty that will keep everyone
On the edge of their seats
For the next two or three years.

Denver

In that frayed summer hat,
She'd pick the strawberries
From our little backyard plot
While the bone-white wave
Of the Rockies
Rose in the background
And broke without a sound.

I'd get the ice and rum
And drop it all together
Into our unpredictable blender.
Now for the bony crunch and hum
Of the blades cutting through
To clearer water.

We sat at the kitchen table
Until our tongues grew numb
With stories that grew ever truer:
Stories of our fathers and mothers.
Elegies for past lovers.
Pencil sketches of things to come.
And our time-proof laughter.

With the last of the daiquiris,
We sat out on the porch stoop
To watch the Rockies
And each other
Disappear.

Pain

Animals in the wild are perfect and know nothing
About pain. Also perfect
Is an Olympic sprinter pulling off
His jersey after a race; the body, flexing
For TV, blinds you; Oh, you say,
That's what it's supposed to look like.
But all wild animals are like this because they live
In a perpetual Olympics. There's no
Margin for error out there,
And any ragged flock of gulls
Surfing a wind current, any rag
Of a jackrabbit poised by the roadside
Dwells in the lean, perfected moment; one
Busted bone, one gray hair, one
Moment's inattention, and he's a goner,
Crunched in the maw of a larger, wilder
Perfection. That's why
They're wild: pain
Never has a chance to teach them
A thing. The parakeet in his cage
Of pain, the ferret on his sexy chain,
Nosing the nipple ring
Of a tattooed punker, the cocker
Spaniel tied by the neck
To the railing outside Starbuck's, waiting
For the slim blonde in the pale
Translucent blouse to finish her latte
With a pale unshaven man she's enjoying

Breaking up with—they're not wild
But bewildered, like us, having learned
From us what pain is, and thus
What it is to be tame, and human.

Wind Turbines

Heading west out of the hills
Above Fremont, the Pacific
Knocking itself senseless in the distance,
You come upon them, an orchard,
A forest, an army of windmills
Marching over the horizon,
Their great props spinning in the sky
As if you'd stumbled upon the propellers
That drive the world's revolution,
Harvesting the wind,
Catching a tidal zephyr by the tail,

Grinding it through the gears,
Cramming it into the mighty, high voltage cables
And firing it down into the distant city
To spin the blades
Of Jasmine's blender
As she whips up the evening's
Third pitcher of margaritas,
The conversation out on the balcony
Just getting interesting, unreal,
Although it's only with a girlfriend,
Also divorced, and they're just about to reach
The point when they raise their glasses
And say, *Fuck 'em all*, by which they mean,
Of course,

Let something smooth and lovely
Slide from the darkness

And into the hungry sockets
Of our bodies, lifting us
Once more to gallop
Through the electrical night
On the wild back of the world.

The Good Kiss

And then there was the night, not long
After my wife had left me and taken on the world-
Destroying fact of a lover, and the city
Roared in flames with it outside my window,
I brought home a nice woman who had listened
To me chant my epic woe for three
Consecutive nights of epic drinking,
Both of us holding on to the bar's
Darkly flowing river of swirling grain
As my own misery flowed past and joined
The tributary of hers, our murmured consolations
Entwining in precisely the same recitative,
The same duet that has been sung
In dark caves of drink since the beginning
Of despair, the song going on
Until there was nothing for it
But to drive through an early summer
Thunderstorm in the windy night
To my little east side apartment
And gently take off her clothes
And lay her down on my bed
By the light of a single candle
And the lightning, and kiss her
For a long time in gratitude
And then desire, and then gently
Kiss the full moons of her breasts,
Which I discovered by candlelight
Were not hers, exactly;
Under each of them was the saddest,

Tenderest little smile of a scar,
Like two sad smiles of apology.
I had them done
So he wouldn't leave, she said,
But in the end he left anyway,
Her breasts standing like two
Cold cathedrals in the light
Of the flaming city, and my lips touched
The little wounds he had left her,
As if a kiss, a good kiss, could heal them,
And I kissed the nipples he had left behind

Until they smoldered like the ashes
Of a campfire the posse finds
Days after the fugitive has slept there
And moved on, drawn by the beautiful
And terrible light of the distant city.

Blues for Cleveland

There's something about middle-aged white guys
Who idolize black jazz and blues musicians
That always makes me uncomfortable.

Charlie Parker, they'll say, pouring the wine.
Bird. Mingus. Oh yeah. They get this
Dreamy, faraway gaze, they exchange

Signs of the brotherhood. *Coleman. Monk.*
Brother Miles. Their wives
Look away, wait for the subject to change.

Outside it's getting dark.
The streetlights flicker into life.
We switch on the security systems.

Laundry

My mother stands in this black
And white arrangement of shadows
In the sunny backyard of her marriage,
Struggling to pin the white ghosts
Of her family on the line.
I watch from my blanket on the grass
As my mother's blouses lift and billow,
Bursting with the day.
My father's white work shirts
Wave their empty sleeves at me,
And my own little shirts and pants
Flap and exult like flags
In the immaculate light.

It is mid-century, and the future lies
Just beyond the white borders
Of this snapshot; soon that wind
Will get the better of her
And her marriage. Soon the future
I live in will break
Through those borders and make
A photograph of her—but

For now the shirts and blouses
Are joyous with her in the yard
As she stands with a wooden clothespin
In her mouth, struggling to keep
The bed sheets from blowing away.

Inherit the Wind

When Mrs. Hoffman, my best friend's mother,
Would pick us up from rehearsals
At the junior high and take us back
To their little apartment
For cookies and milk, she always said
A funny little German phrase
Under her breath as she unlocked
The door and let us in. One day,

We got curious and asked her
What it meant: *Smells like*
A dead Jew in here, she said. *Just*
A saying, and then she lit
A cigarette and sat down
For the evening news, while we
Stuffed ourselves in the kitchen.

Later that spring, I stole one of her bras
As it hung on the line behind the building.
I'd never touched one before. So far,
The closest I'd come was a close inspection
Of the tiny shaking of hands
Between hooks and eyelets just above
The middle vertebrae and beneath
The white blouse of that lovely
Vertebrate, Heather Bailey,
As she sat in front of me taking notes
On the differences between mammals
And reptiles. Now

I sat in my bedroom, flushed with the white
Lace in my hands, hooking
And unhooking it like a quick draw artist,
Imagining a liquid Mrs. Hoffman
Floating in the empty cups.

Was man descended from the apes?
We didn't much care, although the speeches
For God or monkey banged on the rafters
Of the musty theater with all the passion
Our reedy voices could muster. To us
It seemed enough that Heather's breasts
Nodded their secret affirmation
Of the world's essential injustice,
Of life's ineffable anguish and despair,
As she walked across the quad, her hand
In the apish hand of a bruising ninth grader.

Mrs. Hoffman's first husband, Hans,
Had been killed on some front, we knew,
And his body lay for six months in a rail car
On a lonely siding in a bombed-out German town.
But that was ancient history,
And we were living in the now,
In the blank spot, the held breath
Between the fifties
And Vietnam, between
Looking and touching,

And years later, when I was finally able
To unhook a bra with an actual girl in it,
It was as if I'd unlocked

The whole mystery: women were descended
From angels, it was clear. And men—
Men were merely chimps
With clever fingers,
Capable of tearing things apart.

They could ruin things so utterly
That even beautiful Mrs. Hoffman,
After all those years,
Could unlock her stuffy apartment
And still smell Hans in there.

Ike

It's the way they say *Eisenhower*
That makes me tune in
To the two old guys at the next table.

That's how my father said it,
And he hasn't said a word in forty years.
So it's good to know the word
Is still in circulation, like a rare coin,
A first edition.

My father said *Ike*
As if he were nailing down
The precise, original texture of a hot night
In mid-century St. Louis, the sound
As essential to evenings out
On the screened-in porch
As cicadas, crickets, or the Cards
Ebbing and flowing on somebody's radio.

Ike,
He said, with a knowing chuckle
That made it perfectly clear
He knew the man intimately, and liked him.
Ike: a sharp, crew-cut syllable
In which an entire era was compressed
With the terrific density of a star's core,
A sound as open and friendly
As Hopalong Cassidy's wink, a clean keel
Cutting through the fifties, beautifully free

Of the seaweed and barnacles, the faint,
Ironic frisson that would come
To round out the name
Of every politician. My mother

Could say *nigger*
Just as fluently, though never
When the maid was around. She said it
Like she meant it, with an ease
And casual mastery
That embraced an entire history.

Like *Ike,* it's a word
You don't hear much anymore.

Mockingbird

Shriek like a rip
In the dry day. Wry
Imprecation, as the ice cream truck
Disappears around the corner
Of the summer.

The teenager's smile
As she catches me staring
At her halter top.

Gray puff of feathers, gone.

The night manager holding up my time sheet.
The track coach holding up the watch.

Fleet vessel of bone.

My history professor handing back
The essay he hadn't bothered to read and I
Hadn't bothered to write.

The weight inside the halter top.

Squawk like metal
Scraping the day's low-slung chassis

Or hurled down on me
From the TV aerial. The lethal,
Barely perceptible rise
Of my ex-wife's eyebrow.

Gray tail ticking on the phone line.
On the redwood fence. White chevrons
Whirring over the desiccated neighborhood.

A tanned hand
Covering a yawn when I told her
I loved her.

My mother, white-faced
With cancer, asking what my plans were
For the summer.

A hard eye and a sharp beak.

My father putting down his drink
And telling me it was the last time,
With a wink.

Summer's end.
Dead leaves in the dust.

Gray feather
Twirling on a spider's web.

August

Just when you'd begun to feel
You could rely on the summer,
That each morning would deliver
The same mourning dove singing
From his station on the phone pole,
The same smell of bacon frying
Somewhere in the neighborhood,
The same sun burning off
The coastal fog by noon,
When you could reward yourself
For a good morning's work
With lunch at the same little seaside café
With its shaded deck and iced tea,
The day's routine finally down
Like an old song with minor variations,
There comes that morning when the light
Tilts ever so slightly on its track,
A cool gust out of nowhere
Whirlwinds a litter of dead grass
Across the sidewalk, the swimsuits
Are piled on the sale table,
And the back of your hand,
Which you thought you knew,
Has begun to look like an old leaf.
Or the back of someone else's hand.

Nevada

Ten miles from the air base,
Out on the desert floor, is a Quonset hut
Ringed in barbed wire, where the pilots crash-
Land on the whores.

In back, their new Corvettes
And Trans Ams are cooling
Like getaway ponies, while inside
Young guys who spent the day
Carving up the clouds, splitting
The canyons, riding the state
Of the art, are being ancient,
Cracking jokes about cockpits
And joysticks with women

Who might actually find them funny,
Even for the hundredth time, who might
Actually enjoy being flown,
Feeling in some whacked-out way
Like a Phantom, a Corsair, anything
Sounding better than whore,
Although the word is hard
To resist at times, like a handful
Of others in the language
Which serve to provide a base,
A runway, from which we rise,
Eyes wide, head thrown back,
Pulling the heavy G's
Of absolute sin: *whore*

I called her in bed, at the beginning,
In the kind of weird play
Sex can be made of, as if rehearsing
For the time to come

When I called her that
Out of bed and in earnest,

Like these grounded pilots
Describing the wreckage
Of the women they climb out of.

Mysterious Island

My nephew slides
His skinny body into bed,
Shivering a little because it's chilly
And because it just feels so good
To get into bed when you're nine
And your mother's going to read to you
From *The Mysterious Island*
And your big yellow cat leaps up
To his place at the foot of the bed,
Purring with the sheer pleasure
Of the day's lamp-lit ending.

This was my bed, forty years ago,
The little boat I navigated
Through childhood, when the world
Was still perfectly coherent
And nightmares were something
I woke from, and the small universe
Of my room, the house, the yard,
Was so tidy and well-mannered
That being asleep and being awake
Were not so very different—just two
Pleasant, adjoining neighborhoods

I drifted through on my bike
Or my bed until I grew tired
And woke one summer
To that dull sound rising
Beyond the farthest trees,

A muted roar at the edges
Of the neighborhood.
Something about twilight
Was just beginning
To turn me inside out—but
The feeling passed quickly;
My mother cleared her throat,
I closed my eyes. *Now the men*

Are loading their ship
With backpacks and rifles and telescopes.
They are setting out on the dark ocean.

Old Man River

Unable to stand it any longer,
My father got up, made his way
Through the tables in the crowded restaurant
And up to the stage
Where a skinny crooner
Using a microphone to murder
"Old Man River"
Gaped in amazement
As this huge guy, fuelled by five or six
Jack and sodas, joined in
With a baritone not even TB
And a lost lung could entirely destroy,
And made the rafters shake, singing
The goddamn song like it *should* be sung,
The crooner with his shiny mike
Crumpling into silence
Like one of Penelope's suitors,
My mother at the table,
Proud and unembarrassed,
Already planning the divorce.

Divorce

I think of the scene in *Othello,*
After they've traveled
In separate ships through a terrible storm
And come to each other in the dark,
Cavernous hall
In the palace at Cyprus.
It's as if, through some miracle,
They've both been born, or reborn,
At precisely the same moment,
Emerging from the dangerous night
To the sight of each other.

And so the torches are lit;
There is music; life begins.

That's why, walking up the ramp
From the plane at the end of summer,
Home again and heading for the crowded terminal
Where, for the first time, I will not be met,
I think this is what death must be like:
Farewell and departure. The long dark flight,
And arrival in a vast room of smiling strangers
Who have come to meet everyone but you.

Retrospective

For a while
Everything stayed the same;
Time stood still,
Or seemed to, and had
For as long as I could recall.
There was the backyard,
With its dead patch in the shadow.
The cat with its strange meow.
Everything—the doorknobs,
The white clock above the sink,
The open novel (whose title
I can almost read from here)—
Wore that laid-on look, the impasto
Of familiarity.
There was a bolted-down feeling.
Things swung on their hinges
To the right degree, evenings
Came on, and the two of us,
Whoever we were, spoke authentically
Across a little table.
A forest burned somewhere.
The sunsets were appealing.
It was always happening,
Though how I couldn't say.
But there she was, across
A wood-grained table. It might
Have been happiness: a clock
Somewhere clicking reliably.
The light at the end of the day.
And at dawn, geese in the sky.

Cordell

I drove the tiny, grasshopper-green
Motorcycle to the town's edge
And, for the first time,
Bought gas, counting out dimes
And quarters to an old guy in a bill cap.

For the first time,
I pondered the venous skin
Of a map and charted a route from Burns Flat
To Cordell, a little town
On the Oklahoma plains. The day
Was sparkling and unrehearsed, the air
Cool in the morning, and, for the first time,
I went out on the public roads alone,
Despite having no license, the world,
For the first time, passing in a rush
At the tips of the handlebars
On the little country road,
A pick-up passing now and then,
The farmer inside raising the index finger
Of his left hand precisely
An inch above the wheel,
A man greeting me

As a man for the first time,
The little engine whirring under me,
The scissortails watching from barbed wire,
The road unspooling for thirty miles
Just as my map had promised, and, for the first time,

I paused to rest on a long journey,
In this case in the town of Corn,
Its sole street signal
Flashing amber at the crossroads
As I sat at a picnic bench
Under the green dinosaur of the Sinclair station,
Staring at the town and the little bike that took me there,
Feeling, for the first time, like a traveler,
A sojourner of the plains—
And I drove on to Bessie, where,
For the first time, I ordered lunch,
Reading from the menu in a little café,
Speaking seriously and in what I took
To be a manly way, the way of a sojourner,
To the pretty waitress, and what I'd give

Today to see myself sitting there in terror
Amid the half-dozen farmers eating their chicken-
Fried steak, their untanned foreheads white as halos
Above their sunburned faces, and, for the first time,
I left a tip, counting out a silver gift for her,
And walked out to the bike
That waited for me among pick-ups and tractors,
Moving on, for the first time leaving
A woman behind, someone to watch
And acknowledge how the road pulled me away,
Someone to keep on looking down that road

Long after I'd disappeared, someone who might,
From time to time, look toward the window
And brush the hair from her cheek,
Hearing an engine coming from the distance

That swallowed me, for the first time,
That day long ago, a day which for some reason
I am remembering as I sit sipping coffee
In this roadside café, just another rest stop
On the way to Cordell.

Annulment

It's a strange place, that city
Of the people who have forgotten me.
It is not the land of the dead, but
Of the living, which is more terrible.
Boys and girls from old playgrounds
Are growing old there. My best friends
And girlfriends, my fellow drones
At the restaurant, the retail stores,
In Boy Scouts, on the track team,
At the language school in Japan,
The cast of thousands who knew me
And laughed with me and had a beer
Or two with me after work, and confessed
To me their perfectly valid realities
As I confessed mine in turn, our lies
And stories mingling, becoming our lives—
They're mowing the lawn now, or sitting
At a desk, or worrying about their marriages,
Or just walking idly along
In that small city of those who have forgotten me,
Or nearly have, my name sometimes
Gusting across the wide yard of memory
Like a dead leaf, raising a smile,
Or a twinge of regret, or anger,
Or nothing much at all, as their lives
Go on with less of me
By the minute, in that bustling town
I cannot find, somewhere on the plains
Where she is traveling now,
Drawing closer to it every day.

About the Author

George Bilgere is the author of two previous collections of poetry, *The Going* (University of Missouri Press) and *Big Bang* (Copper Beech Press). His poems have appeared in such periodicals and anthologies as *Poetry, Sewanee Review, The Southern Review, Ploughshares, The Kenyon Review,* and *The Best American Poetry.* A recipient of fellowships from the National Endowment for the Arts, the Fulbright Commission, the Witter Bynner Foundation, and the Ohio Arts Council, he is a professor of English at John Carroll University in Cleveland, Ohio.

About the Book

The Good Kiss was designed and typeset by Amy Freels.
The cover was designed and typeset by Jodi Gabor.

The Good Kiss was printed on 60-pound Natural and bound by BookMasters of Ashland, Ohio.